CLAIRE TREVOR

A One-Person Play in Two Acts
By

Michael B. Druxman

The Hollywood Legends

TIME & PLACE

ACT I

1968: The living room of Claire Trevor's Newport Beach home.

ACT II

1980: The living room of Claire Trevor's Newport Beach home.

SETTING

The living room of Claire Trevor's Newport Beach home.

Entrance to the room is UL; also access to the rest of the house.

Functional furnishings include an armchair, sofa, coffee and end tables, and a wet bar.

An Academy Award statuette sits on one of the tables.

CLAIRE TREVOR

ACT I

AT RISE: CLAIRE TREVOR, *late 50s, sits in the armchair, talking on the telephone. Her figure is trim; her hair champagne-blonde. She is dressed in an attractive, not inexpensive, blouse and skirt.*

CLAIRE TREVOR
(*Into Phone:*)

I quit.

Left the tour in Chicago.

I shouldn't have done the damn play in the first place.

Hermione Baddeley….

She's replacing me.

Hell, I was already "retired" when they offered it to me.

I should have stayed retired.

Why'd I do it?

I was getting too damn comfortable…

Milton thought I should do it….

Besides…

The Killing of Sister George…

It was a hit in London…New York…

So, I decided to stir things up.

Do something different for me.

I added a British accent…

Dressed up like Oliver Hardy.

I'll admit…

It *was* "different" playing a cigar-smoking lesbian.

(*Chuckles*)

Actually, I'm not sure it was a compliment that they even thought of me for that role….

It really wasn't a good fit.

Your memory gets lazy in the movies.

I haven't been on stage for ten years….

And, I only had three weeks to learn the script.

My reviews weren't good.

I know…

Not the best vehicle to end one's career on.

So now, I'm *really* retired.

I'll concentrate on my painting…

Let's have lunch next week.

She hangs up the phone.

(To herself)
What happened to the parts I would have given my soul for?

The ones that Bette Davis got?

She gets up; looks about the room; moves the Oscar statuette to a more prominent place on the table.

She becomes aware of the audience.

Hello.

I didn't realize you were here.

Actually, I'm glad you are.

You heard that…

So, you know my career has probably come to an end.

It's been a good career….

Not exactly the career I would have wanted, but…

Maybe if I talk to you…

I can figure out what went wrong.

Milton…

Milton Bren, my husband…

He's heard all these stories a million times.

With you…hopefully…they'll be fresh.

Ponders, then:

I've played everything in movies…

Over sixty of them.

I was the "Queen of Film Noir".

That's right!

I was typed…more or less…

As a streetwalker…

The girl of ill repute…

The gangster's moll.

The shady lady…

The fallen woman.

Every movie was shot in eighteen days,

You'd work every Saturday night.

You'd have an hour for dinner….

And, you'd work until two or three in the morning.

Some of it wasn't easy….

But, a lot of those movies were good because they were made fast.

And….

Back in the days when I was doing those pictures, you could still keep your clothes on.

I was still a nice Jewish girl from Bensonhurst in Brooklyn…

Whose parents moved to Larchmont, New York, shortly after I was born.

My father was the best custom-tailor in New York.

My mother was also a skilled dressmaker.

Where do you think I got my appreciation for quality clothes?

I could have gone to Smith… Vassar….

I decided that was too much trouble.

Instead, I attended the American Academy of Dramatic Arts.

It was a whim, but…

I was only there a short time when they handed me the difficult role of the child in Ibsen's *The Wild Duck*.

I was a miserable failure…

I decided to give up all thoughts of theatre then and there.

But, friends talked me into trying again.

Why not?

What else did I have to do?

I spent two six-month terms at the Academy.

After that is when you do the Shakespeare plays.

Why did I need Shakespeare?

I felt that if I got out and worked and got a job, I'd learn more.

I made my *professional* stage debut in 1929 in Ann Arbor, Michigan.

I had one line in a production of *Lady Windermere's Fan*.

"*Yes, Mama*".

What did you expect?

Hamlet's soliloquy?

Then, the Depression came along…

My father's Fifth Avenue business went bust…

He'd dressed all the important men who jumped out of a window during the crash.

And, I *had* to go to work.

I modeled.

I looked for acting jobs.

I was so green.

I didn't know you had to study for a part.

I thought you just went on and did the best you could.

I started appearing in one and two-reel Vitaphone shorts.

They were terrible!

But, they got me noticed.

I got hired by a stock company in St. Louis…

We did everything; even made the scenery.

It was one of the best summers I've ever had in my life.

That led to me being signed by Metro-Goldwyn-Mayer for three months…

Which led nowhere.

I was twenty-two…

I did another play…

Whistling in the Dark….

Which was a hit!

M.G.M. was interested in me again.

They'd bought the screen rights to the play.

Irving Thalberg offered me a seven-year contract.

I told him I preferred to remain on the stage.

He didn't believe I was serious.

He took an hour trying to convince me I was making a mistake.

I still said "*No*" … and I've hated myself ever since.

So, Una Merkel played my role in *Whistling in the Dark*...

And, I went back to New York and looked for work for the next few months.

There wasn't any.

And then, out of the blue…

I got an offer from Fox.

I was a blonde…and they were looking for another Mae West.

After a star becomes famous like Mae West, it isn't difficult to find others to mimic her well…

But, who wants to see imitations?

I signed the contract…

I needed the money.

Fox didn't know it then…

They weren't going to get "Mae West".

They were going to get "Claire Trevor".

Before we go any further, I should clear something up.

My real name is "Claire Wemlinger".

I know. That doesn't look good on a marquee.

I saw a sign: *Sinclair Oil.*

I decided to call myself "*Clair Sinclair*".

Then, I started using "*Clair St. Clair*".

Later, I was in some agent's office and he took a telephone book…put his finger down randomly on a page.

And, that's how I became "*Claire Trevor*".

My father was so strict, he insisted that my mother accompany me to Hollywood and live with me there.

She was ready for anything.

She adored being on the set.

When we had to work until two or three in the morning, she was thrilled.

For her, it was a party.

For me, it was a pain in the ass…

Literally.

I'd never ridden a horse before, and I had to learn…fast.

Fox had cast me in two Westerns with George O'Brien.

You've never heard of them.

But, I fell madly in love with George, and thought he was one of the most charming men I'd ever met.

When he told me he was about to get married, I was crushed.

Another picture you've never heard of…

The Mad Game.

But, this one starred Spencer Tracy.

Tracy was very, very impressed with me

That sounds braggadocio, but it's the truth.

He liked the way I delivered lines; tossed my lines away.

He really liked my style.

He even asked me out.

I was tempted…but then I told him:

"*I don't go out with married men.*".

He smiled, and said: "*Stay that way.*".

At Fox….

Darryl Zanuck kept casting me in these "quickies' that are long gone and forgotten.

Twenty-two of them.

The second features on double-bills.

Ever hear of *Wild Gold*?

Spring Tonic?

I didn't think so.

I could never push myself.

It was my own non-fighting nature that kept me from going after the really important roles.

That…and I didn't cooperate with the studio publicity department.

In those days, every actress had a label.

I didn't want to be known as "*The Ear*" or "*The Toe*".

On the other hand, Fox was certainly a good training ground.

Aside from Tracy, I worked with Lew Ayres…

Brian Donlevy…

Cesar Romero…

Gilbert Roland…

Jimmy Dunn….

In 1937, I was sent over to Samuel Goldwyn's studio to meet William Wyler.

He was directing a film version of the hit stage play, *Dead End.*

"*At last,*" I thought, "*I'll get to work with a great director.*"

So, the first thing he says to me is:

"*Tell me, Miss Trevor, what have you done*?"

I was destroyed.

I knew I was no Garbo, but I had starred in twenty-two "B" pictures, and Wyler hadn't seen any of them.

He was just interviewing me at Samuel Goldwyn's suggestion.

Then, when he offered me a role that was only two pages long in the script, I was really hurt.

I went home and read the part.

It was "Francey"....

A sweet young girl who had turned into a pitiful, hardened prostitute.

Of course, back in 1937, we couldn't say her profession...only suggest it.

I was tired of doing routine heroines in routine romances.

I needed something to give me a break...and "Francey" was the answer.

Wyler was marvelously meticulous.

He shuffled through the entire wardrobe department and picked out my dress himself.

I wore no makeup...

Just some eye makeup and some lipstick…

That was it.

I felt dirty and run-down and awful when I did that scene with Humphrey Bogart…

…and it was marvelous.

I wish that scene had gone on forever.

I got my first Oscar nomination for *Dead End.*

I thought, "*Maybe now I can get into 'A' pictures, because* Dead End *was an 'A' picture; a very big picture.*"

It didn't happen.

Zanuck put me back into "B"s.

He never had faith in me.

Why, I don't know.

So, when the opportunity arose, I quit Fox.

Went freelance.

I wasn't totally without income.

Thanks to *Dead End*, I had a radio show.

Did it for three years.

"*Big Town*"

Edward G. Robinson played a crusading newspaper editor, and I was "Lorelei," his "girl Friday".

I also married, Clark Andrews, the show's producer.

He was a Yale graduate.

He liked tennis.

I liked tennis.

The marriage was over in four years.

Aside from his paying too much attention to other women…

The bastard had to borrow money from me to settle his bills.

Okay…

You want me to talk about *Stagecoach.*

John Ford…

I didn't want to go see him when he asked to see me for *Stagecoach.*

I had fever blisters on my face from the sun.

It was swollen.

I went to his set…

He was shooting a submarine picture…

And, I held a hanky over my face the whole time.

That aside….

I believed in John Ford completely.

Whatever he said, I would have done.

If he had said to me:

"Claire, walk down to the edge of the cliff and at the signal jump off."

I would have said "*Okay*".

That's how much I trusted him.

He was spellbinding.

(*Chuckles*)

Okay, I'm not that crazy.

We were in Monument Valley.

I wouldn't have jumped off a cliff….

In *Stagecoach*, I played "Dallas," the dance hall girl.

In 1939 movies, we were "dance hall girls," not prostitutes.

Thomas Mitchell was in the cast…

He won an Oscar…

John Carradine… Andy Devine…

He was the stage driver.

And, of course, the new guy…John Wayne.

He got the part after Joel McCrea turned it down.

Ford liked to bully his actors.

One day, he said to Andy Devine:

"*You big tub of lard. I don't know why the hell I'm using you in this picture!*"

And Andy replied:

"*Because Ward Bond can't drive six horses.*"

(*Chuckles*)

Ford was worse on Wayne.

He kept calling him a "*big oaf*" and a "*dumb bastard*"….

One day, he grabbed Duke by the chin and shook him.

He said: "*Why are you moving your mouth so much?*

"*Don't you know you don't act with your mouth in pictures?*

"*You act with your eyes.*"

Ford may have been right....

But, it's amazing how Duke tolerated that kind of treatment.

Duke and I had a chemistry that came across on film.

We like each other in real life and are great friends.

We both live in Newport Beach.

Some people thought we must be having an affair, but that wasn't so.

Duke liked dark Latin types, and I was blonde.

I was the highest paid cast member on *Stagecoach*.

Fifteen thousand dollars.

Duke only got thirty-seven hundred.

Even Tim Holt...the cavalry officer...

He got five thousand.

How times have changed.

(*Chuckles*)

Louise Platt…

She played the very proper pregnant wife in *Stagecoach.*

Off-screen, she wasn't quite as proper.

One day, she was looking at Duke, and she said to me:

"*I think he has the most beautiful buttocks I've ever seen.*"

Ponders, then:

When *Stagecoach* was released….

My agent was out of town for six months.

Nobody was around to pursue better roles for me.

Ponders, then:

I did a couple pictures with George Raft….

A couple more with Duke…

They were just crummy.

Then, I did *Honky Tonk* with Clark Gable.

Lana Turner was the lead.

I was the…

What else…!

The hard-boiled dance hall girl.

Gable was so wonderful.

To me, he was very adolescent.

Sweet, sort of naïve in a way.

My costume…

I had on black net stockings and a short sort of thing.

He looked over at me, and went "*Woo-woo-woo*".

Just what you'd expect of him.

I was so upset when I went to see *Honky Tonk*.

Most of my role had been cut from the picture.

I started to cry, and I don't cry easily.

I couldn't stop crying.

I thought:

"I hate this business. I hate it, and I'm through with it. I don't want to do it anymore."

I didn't quit.

I did a couple pictures with Glenn Ford…

My first with Randolph Scott…

And, *Street of Chance* with Burgess Meredith.

I played a double-dealing *femme fatale.*

It wasn't "Lady MacBeth"….

I would have loved to have played her.

But, it was my introduction to *film noir.*

Ponders then:

In 1943, I got married again.

Lt. Cylos William Dunsmoore.

He was a Navy pilot.

I wanted to be a housewife, but I was hopeless in the kitchen.

We have a son, Charles.

From childhood on, I wanted children.

Even babies in strangers' baby carriages appealed to me.

If the maternal part of my nature hadn't been satisfied, I'd have felt like a failure in life.

I considered myself lucky…

For having a child.

But, the marriage ended in 1946.

My husband was morose…sulky.

He didn't try to find a job after he left the service.

And, he used profanity.

Fuck him!

What a holler would ensue if people had to pay the minister as much to marry them as they have to pay a lawyer to get them a divorce.

Ponders, then:

The next *important* movie I did was *Murder, My Sweet.*

Eddie Dmytryk directed.

It was an adaptation of Raymond Chandler's novel, *Farewell, My Lovely.*

I played the double-dealing *femme fatale* again.

Dick Powell starred as “Philip Marlowe”.

The problem was that, until then, Powell had always appeared in musicals.

Remember *Gold Diggers of 1933*?

1935?

Footlight Parade?

Nobody saw him as a hard-boiled private detective.

But, he was great in the role.

Gave him a whole new career as a tough guy.

They *did*, however, change that title of the picture to *Murder, My Sweet* after the first preview.

With Powell as the star, audiences thought that *Farewell, My Lovely* was going to be a musical.

I did another Broadway play.

It closed after twenty-one performances.

That was the finest thing that could have happened to me.

The Broadway mirage was gone.

I had always said that I didn't want to be a movie star, and I meant it.

Didn't I turn down Thalberg?

I woke up to the truth.

I decided to try to be a Hollywood star.

Movie stars have such advantages.

Born to Kill.

Another *film noir*.

They originally wanted Tallulah Bankhead, but I got the part.

Robert Wise…

He was still somewhat a novice when he directed, this one, but boy was he good.

I was thrilled to work with him.

My co-star, Lawrence Tierney….

He tended to be a bit unstable at times…

I'm not sure he ever got over playing "John Dillinger".

I was really perverted in *Born to Kill.*

There's a scene where I discover that Tierney has just killed a couple people.

I decide not to call the cops.

I say:

"It's a lot of bother, coroner's inquests and all that stuff."

(*Chuckles*)

I've never known any woman as bad as the ones I've played on the screen.

Even my family was getting ashamed of me.

A gun factory even wanted to name a new pocket pistol after me.

I did another *noir*….

Raw Deal with Dennis O'Keefe.

And then, I got married again.

Number three was the charm.

Milton is a producer.

He did a couple of the *Topper* movies….

Two pictures with Wallace Beery.

And, he's a genius when it comes to real estate.

He built office buildings on Sunset Boulevard near Doheny.

We have a good life.

We have our boat…

The Lady Claire….

We have our kids….

Until I really knew Milton, I had an inferiority complex.

I was in a rut.

But, he brought me out of it.

He would say:

"*Would you like me to read your script and help you?*"

He picked *Key Largo* for me.

Remember that cast?

Humphrey Bogart…

Edward G. Robinson…

Lauren Bacall…

Lionel Barrymore…

I'd read the script and agreed with him.

I knew I'd be right for "Gaye Dawn".

She was the former singer who'd become Eddie Robinson's alcoholic girl friend.

I really wanted that role.

Unfortunately, the bosses at Warner Bros. didn't want to pay me my regular salary.

They figured that one of their contract players could be had for less.

That's when, Milton took over.

He knew that our friend, Bogie, wanted me for the part.

He decided to work on him.

They were in a steam room together.

And, Milton started to needle Bogie.

"*You're no big star,*" he said.

"*If you had any influence with Jack Warner, you'd insist that Claire play the part.*"

Bogie started getting defensive, but Milton didn't let up.

"*If you had any guts, you'd pick up the phone right now and tell Warner that if Claire doesn't do the film, neither will you.*

That went on for about an hour.

Then, Bogie called Warner and, later that afternoon, I was cast in the part.

That was the first time I'd ever gone after an important role…

And, it paid off.

My character was based on a real-life gangster's moll, Gay Orlova.

She was Lucky Luciano's girl friend.

John Huston was our director.

Early on, I asked him for some insight into the character.

He said: "*You're the kind of drunken dame whose eyebrows are always a little too big….*

"*Your voice is a little too loud….*

"*And, you're a little too polite.*

"*You're very sad, very resigned.*"

I'm no trained singer….

And, in one scene, I had to sing "*Moanin' Low*" … a capella

That's without instrumental accompaniment.

All along, Huston, assured me that I would be lip-syncing to someone else's voice.

Still, I was nervous about that scene.

I wanted to rehearse….

But, he kept putting me off.

"*There's plenty of time,*" he said.

Then, one day…out of the blue…

He told me that they were going to shoot the song now…

Without any rehearsal.

That son-of-a-bitch!

I was given my starting note from the piano…

Then, in front of the cast and crew…

I sang the song.

I was hesitant…uncomfortable….

I was supposed to be horrible.

That's the take they used in the film.

And, that's the scene that won me the Academy Award for 1948.

Best Actress in a Supporting Role.

When that happens….

There's sort of an explosion which makes you half deaf and blind.

Somehow you find yourself on the stage and you begin to hear the applause.

It was a glorious night.

The after party….

The congratulations….

And, the next morning….

It was over.

Producers weren't breaking down my door to sign me for their next big budget picture.

For a while, they weren't calling at all.

She ponders a bit, as:

LIGHTS FADE

END OF ACT ONE

ACT II

AT RISE: *It's twelve years later.*

Little has changed in the room, except there are some packing boxes scattered about.

TREVOR, now 70, *sits in her armchair, talking on the phone. She is dressed in different blouse and skirt.*

CLAIRE TREVOR
(*Into Phone:*)

I'm leaving next week.

New surroundings….

Old friends…

It will help.

I might even travel.

Of course, I'd love to work.

I should have done *Agnes of God* when they offered it to me.

Wonderful play.

Finally, I could have been it a hit.

I just didn't feel like doing anything that heavy then.

But, I don't have an agent now…

And, I don't really know many people in the business any more.

I *know* I still have a "name"….

If people still remember it.

I haven't done anything for over four years.

I'll call you before I go.

She hangs up the phone; looks about.

She puts a couple of items into boxes, then becomes aware of the audience.

You're back.

You always seem to drop in when I've got issues.

Today, you've got a home run.

The easy one is that I'm moving to New York.

Great apartment there.

Four bedrooms…three baths...high ceilings….

It's better to have more space, than not enough.

I'm hoping that'll help me deal with the other issues.

But, you're not going to appreciate *why* I'm moving to New York unless you know who's on the other three bases

(*Chuckles*)

Who's on first?

Sounds like an Abbott and Costello routine, doesn't it?

Don't worry.

I'll get to the other "issues" ….

But, first…

We ought to do a little catch-up.

The last time we talked….

I'd just won the Oscar, right?

(*Chuckles*)

A couple nights before the Academy Awards that year, Bogie and Betty…

That's Lauren Bacall….

They were over for dinner.

And, Bogie said:

"Listen kid, if you win, I want you to get up and say:

"'I'm not going to thank anybody. I did it all myself'"
(*Chuckles*)
I really didn't think that would ingratiate me to anyone.

After I won, if you read the Hollywood trade papers…

You'd have thought I was going to do every picture in town.

Any Number Can Play with Gable.

Flamingo Road with Joan Crawford.

They didn't happen.

It was all press agent bullshit.

What did I do?

The Babe Ruth Story with William Bendix.

Bill had been a bat boy at Yankee Stadium during the early 1920s.

He had personally seen Ruth hit over 100 home runs.

That was why he wanted to do the picture.

Me?

I'd been stuck in such a series of grim, hard-boiled parts....

I was tickled silly when the Babe's life gave me the chance to play a successful normal human being at last.

My reviews were okay...

But, most critics didn't like the picture...

And, they sure didn't like Bendix as the great Babe Ruth.

Some called it "*the worst sports movie ever made*".

So, I went back to *noir*.

I did *The Lucky Stiff* with Brian Donlevy...

Like a fool, I turned down *Caged*, the woman's prison picture....

The one with Eleanor Parker....

That's a minor classic.

And Shelly Winters beat me out of *Winchester .73* with Jimmy Stewart.

Milton, my dear husband, came to my rescue.

He produced *Borderline.*

I did it with Fred MacMurray…Raymond Burr….

It was set in Mexico, but we shot it in Chatsworth.

Fred and I played undercover cops.

Neither one of us knew the other was undercover, which added to the fun.

I had an accident on that picture.

Slipped…hurt my foot…

And, I had to do a dance routine.

But, I kept working.

A first aid attendant massaged my foot and put ice packs on the swollen area.

Fred, Milton and I weren't taking salaries for this picture.

We were all working for a percentage of the profits.

I'll be damned if I was going to let it go over budget.

After *Borderline…*

I did *Hard, Fast and Beautiful.*

Ida Lupino directed.

She's such a talented lady.

But, she's intense and emotional.

I don't react well to that type of person.

I balked.

I went home…

Told Milton that she was going to drive me crazy with all her dramatic talk.

But, she knows more about directing than a lot of men.

She's really a very warm…very sensitive and intelligent lady.

Hard, Fast and Beautiful was about a tennis champion…

Sally Forrest…

Who is being exploited by her ambitious mother.

Me!

Stop, You're Killing Me….

That was a semi-musical remake of an old Edward G. Robinson picture, *A Slight Case of Murder.*

A Damon Runyon comedy.

Broderick Crawford played the Robinson part, and I was his wife.

It was in color…but the original was better.

Another Randolph Scott western…

Then, I went over to "the enemy camp".

Made my television debut.

An episode of "Ford Theatre".

It allowed me to do what I couldn't do in pictures:

Play a sympathetic, normal role.

In 1954, I got my third Academy Award nomination.

The High and the Mighty.

It was one of the first airline disaster movies.

John Wayne…Robert Stack…Jan Sterling…Laraine Day….

I played a warm-hearted *kept* woman who, during the tenuous flight from Hawaii, falls in love with David Brian.

Filming that picture was a big bore.

Never do an airplane movie.

Even if we didn't have any lines or anything to do, we had to be sitting in that plane for almost every damn shot.

I didn't win the Oscar.

I didn't expect to.

Eva Marie Saint did.

That was the year of *On the Waterfront*.

I did a Western with Kirk Douglas…

Played another of my wise-cracking saloon keepers.

Lucy Gallant…

That was about women's fashion, with Jane Wyman and Charlton Heston….

My character's name in that one was "Lady Macbeth".

Still not Shakespeare's lady….

A year later…

I won an Emmy Award.

Fredric March and I did Sidney Howard's "Dodsworth" as an "NBC Producers Showcase Production.

I also did another movie with Spencer Tracy. *The Mountain.*

Oh, God, that was a terrible picture!

It goes on forever…and it's bad.

Robert Wagner looked like he was twelve years old…and he's playing Tracy's brother.

Spence had already gotten heavy and old looking.

He was "on the wagon" when he consented to do the film, but…

On the way up to the resort where they were staying…

Their cable car malfunctioned…and they were stuck in that scary situation for some time.

The experience caused Spence to drink heavily that night…

Hell, after that experience, *I* would have drunk heavily that night.

You didn’t want to be around Spence when he was drinking.

He lost his temper.

He threw a glass at the bartender.

The glass didn't hit the man…

But, it shattered and pieces of it cut Bob Wagner's hand.

The whole experience on that picture was miserable…ludicrous.

I really missed doing theatre.

They’d offered me ten week tours of *The Country Girl…*

A Streetcar Named Desire…

Who wouldn’t want to play “Blanche DuBois”?

But, I had a young son at home.

I was even thinking of retirement.

What was all this about anyway?

The fame was nonsense.

I'd been to all the parties I wanted to go to and had the social chi-chi.

I thought of Marilyn Monroe and Elizabeth Taylor…

I didn't want to deal with all the emotional effects they had to endure.

Ponders, then:

Two years later, I did *Marjorie Morningstar.*

It was adapted from the Herman Wouk novel.

I was Natalie Wood's Jewish mother.

Gene Kelly was in it…Everett Sloane…

Natalie reminded me of myself when I was her age.

She was rushing from picture to picture.

And, she'd been acting since she was four.

All her time was spent with older people.

Where was her childhood?

Four years after that, I was Edward G. Robinson's wife in *Two Weeks in Another Town.*
(*Chuckles*)

I'm his mistress in *Key Largo*...and now I'm his wife.

And, in this one, I was a first-class bitch.

Kirk Douglas was the star.

The Stripper with Joanne Woodward....

Marilyn Monroe was supposed to have starred in that one, but....

We'd lost her by then.

The Stripper was adapted from a William Inge play:

A Loss of Roses.

Sort of an ironic title, isn't it?

In 1967, I went to South Africa and did *The Cape Town Affair*.

James Brolin and Jacqueline Bisset were the stars.

I played a bag lady in that one.

I don't want you to get the idea that, between pictures, I wasn't working.

Remember television?

I did episodes of "Alfred Hitchcock Presents" ....

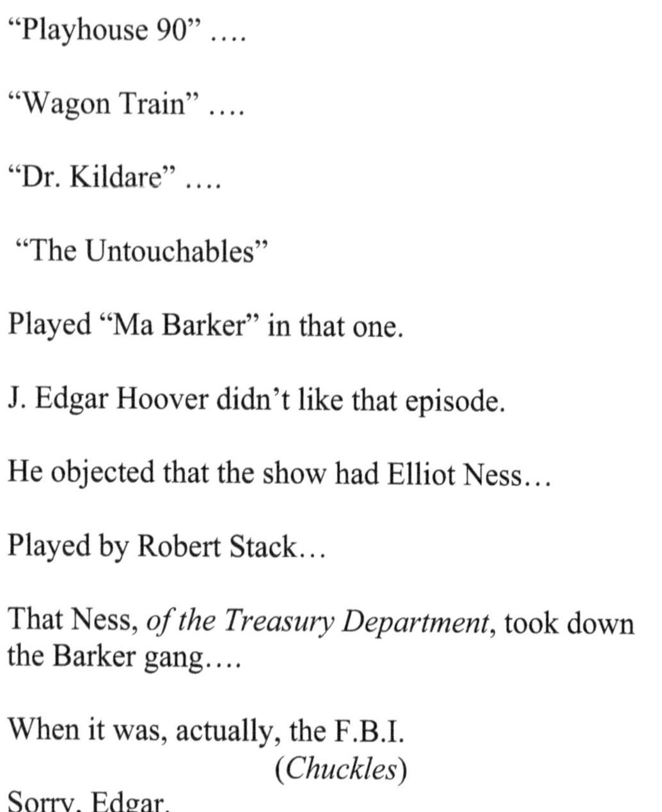

"Playhouse 90" ….

"Wagon Train" ….

"Dr. Kildare" ….

"The Untouchables"

Played "Ma Barker" in that one.

J. Edgar Hoover didn't like that episode.

He objected that the show had Elliot Ness…

Played by Robert Stack…

That Ness, *of the Treasury Department*, took down the Barker gang….

When it was, actually, the F.B.I.
(*Chuckles*)
Sorry, Edgar.

Ponders, then:

I did go back on the stage in 1976.

I'd been away for eight years.

It was a revival of *John Brown's Body*, the Civil War verse play by Stephen Vincent Benet.

I did it with Rock Hudson…Leif Erickson….

John Houseman directed it.

Our reviews were good…but the audiences weren't there.

The producers didn't know what they were doing.

They'd booked us into college campuses during the summer.

We were playing to empty houses.

After we played Denver, they cancelled the rest of the tour.

And now, I'm going to New York.

And, it's time, I guess, to talk about the other issues.

The triple play.

Two years ago….

She stars to weep.

My son, Charles….

He was killed in the Pacific Southwest airplane disaster over San Diego.

The following year….

My dear friend….

John Wayne died.

I'm sure you all felt that loss.

Then, last December….

She cries for a long moment.

Milton died.

He was seventy-five.

Had a brain tumor.

Wipes her eyes.
Ponders, then:

After the skies opened up and fell on me….

I tried to eliminate a lot of memories that were painful.

New York will be a good change.

I was never very extravagant.

I supported my parents during the Depression.

And, I saved my money.

Not that I deprived myself….

I mean, if I needed a fur coat, I'd get it.

(*Chuckles*)
Doesn't every woman *need* a fur coat?

But, in spite of the roles I played, I didn't go wild.

So, I'm going wild now.

Not bad exactly….

Just a little wild.

I *did* make a large donation…

And, I do mean large….

To the University of California Irvine Theater.

Milton left me very well off.

Ponders, then:

I don't watch my movies any more.

They edit them on television…and add commercials.

And, it is kind of a jolt to see yourself.

I'd rather remember *Stagecoach* and *Key Largo* than see them.

I have my painting.

I've done portraits of Tyrone Power…Lauren Bacall….

I worked hard at it.

I forged ahead in painting and outgrew my art class.

It had become more of a social thing.

To me, acting and painting are closely related.

You need imagination for both.

I don't know how good my paintings are….

Nor, do I care.

I'm going to fill my hours with pleasure….

And, you can't take that away.

Painting is a lot cheaper than going to a psychiatrist.

I'd better get back to my packing.

If you're in New York, come see me.

She resumes packing the boxes.

LIGHTS FADE

ANNOUNCER

Claire Trevor made one more film after moving to New York, as well as doing a couple of episodic television shows.

She died on April 8, 2000.

She was ninety years old.

CLAIRE TREVOR (*V.O.*)

Some people have it…

That flair for the spectacular.

But, I'm not one of them.

It would be ridiculous for me to try it.

So, I'll never be "good copy," will I?

THE END

THE HOLLYWOOD LEGENDS is a series of one and two-person, two-act plays by Hollywood biographer, historian, screenwriter and playwright Michael B. Druxman that explore the life and times of some of filmdom's most glittering personalities.

From Clara Bow, "The 'It' Girl" of the silent era, through the birth of the talkies with Al Jolson and Maurice Chevalier, on through the thirties and forties with superstars like Clark Gable, Spencer Tracy, Carole Lombard, Errol Flynn, Basil Rathbone, Jeanette MacDonald and Nelson Eddy, Ida Lupino, Dick Powell, Clifton Webb, Yvonne De Carlo, Gary Cooper, Audrey Hepburn, Roy Scheider, Jason Robards, Larry Parks, Bud Abbott, Maureen O'Hara, Abe Vigoda, Christopher Lee, Ronald Reagan, Ethel Barrymore, Charlton Heston, and, finally, Hollywood's "boy genius," Orson Welles, these anecdote-filled dramatic pieces present a humorous, often touching portrait of each star and the era in which he/she lived.

The collection has now been expanded to include multiple character plays like: LANA & JOHNNY WERE LOVERS (Lana Turner), SEXY REXY (Rex Harrison). B MOVIE, which deals with the Franchot Tone/ Barbara Payton/Tom Neal scandal of the 1950s, ROBINSON & RAFT (Edward G. Robinson, George Raft), THE LAST MONSTERS (Bela Lugosi, Lon Chaney, Jr. & John Carradine), AVA & HER GUYS (Ava Gardner, Mickey Rooney, Artie Shaw, Frank Sinatra), BRODERICK CRAWFORD, and CLOWNS ON THE GROUND (Milton Berle, Joe E. Brown, Bert Lahr).

The plays, many of which have seen several productions, utilize simple costumes and props, and are designed to be staged on a single setting, with shifts in lighting to denote changes in time and place.

All questions with regard to licensing should be addressed to the author: Michael B. Druxman, PMB 119, 4301 W. William Cannon Dr., Suite B-150, Austin, TX 78749 [*druxy@ix.netcom.com*].

www.ingramcontent.com/pod-product-compliance
Ingram Content Group UK Ltd.
Pitfield, Milton Keynes, MK11 3LW, UK
UKHW021651190726
13853UKWH00001B/189